ZERO-BASE BUDGETING: ORGANIZATIONAL IMPACT AND EFFECTS

an AMA survey report

L. Allan Austin

A DIVISION OF AMERICAN MANAGEMENT ASSOCIATIONS

Library of Congress Cataloging in Publication Data

Austin, L   Allan.
    Zero-base budgeting.

    (An AMA survey report)
    Bibliography: p.
    1. Zero-base budgeting. 2. Budget in business.
I. Title. II. Series: American Management Associa-
tions. An AMA survey report.
HF5550.A88   658.1'54   77-25831
ISBN 0-8144-3130-5

Contents

Section		Page
1	Survey Purpose and Findings	1
2	The Zero-Base Budgeting Process	4
3	Characteristics and Responses of Organizations Implementing ZBB	12
4	Special Needs and Considerations in Implementing ZBB	18
5	Benefits and Limitations of the ZBB Process	23
	Appendix Samples of Decision Packages from the Watervliet Paper Company	27
	References	31
	Bibliography	32

Selected Exhibits

1.	Organizations by Stage of ZBB Implementation	12
7.	Organizational Level of ZBB Implementation	15
8.	Implementing Respondents by Title	15
9.	Most Significant Reason for Implementing ZBB	15
12.	Resource Shifts Resulting from ZBB Implementation	16
13.	Impact of ZBB Implementation on Corporate Profitability	16
14.	Effect of ZBB Implementation on Time and Effort Required in Budget Preparation	17

About the Author

L. Allan Austin is Partner in the management consulting firm of Austin & Lindberg, Ltd. of Salt Lake City, Utah.

Mr. Austin has held a number of positions on the academic staff of the University of Utah. He taught courses in economics, finance, management, educational psychology, and social work. He speaks on the subject of zero-base planning and budgeting in this country and abroad and specializes in designing and installing ZBB systems.

Mr. Austin was employed for three years by the Federal Home Loan Bank Board in Washington, D.C., where he had responsibilities for organizational development and planning.

He has written extensively in the business field; his publications include several articles and two co-authored books.

Mr. Austin was born and raised in the Far East.

Basis of the Research

The material for this survey report was gathered principally from questionnaires and a telephone survey administered to 481 enterprises that have been using zero-base budgeting and/or have attended zero-base budgeting seminars conducted by the American Management Associations. Conducted during the spring of 1977, the survey generated 223 replies—a 46 percent response rate.

Acknowledgments

The author wishes to thank both the people who helped design the survey—Joseph Bentley, Logan Cheek, Henry H. Goldman, Peter Pyhrr, Thomasine Rendero, and Philip Vrzal—and the staff of Austin and Lindberg, Ltd., who helped gather and process the data.

1
Survey Purpose and Findings

No U.S. Presidential campaign ever affected specific business methods as much as the last one. One of the planks in Jimmy Carter's presidential election platform was his experience with zero-base planning and budgeting (ZBB) and his intention to introduce the method in the federal government. Shortly after he was elected, bills were submitted to both Houses of Congress calling for adoption of the technique by the federal government. Interest in zero-base budgeting since then has exploded.

A front-page feature in the March 11, 1977, issue of *The Wall Street Journal* heralded the zero-base budgeting process as the latest advancement in management practice. The article noted that Peter Pyhrr's book, *Zero-Base Budgeting* (John Wiley & Sons, 1973), was then selling at the rate of 700 copies per week, despite its price ($19.25) and its age (four years). The first printing of a new book by Logan M. Cheek, *Zero-Base Budgeting Comes of Age* (AMACOM, 1977), sold out soon after its publication.

Great Expectations

The rise of interest in zero-base budgeting is such that administrators in every sector of the economy are being pressed to study and/or implement the technique. And, because organizations tend to implement major changes in conformity with current interests in the management field—exemplified in recent years by performance standards, management by objectives, job enrichment, and organizational development—many organizations will install ZBB systems with the expectation that major benefits will follow. However, little empirical evidence supporting that expectation has been produced; not much hard data on ZBB implementation exists in the public domain. Therefore, the possible impact of implementation on a company's performance cannot be well understood in advance. To proceed without such understanding can jeopardize the success of implementation or reduce the effectiveness of the process after installation.

Purpose of the Study

The primary purpose of this study is to provide administrators with information helpful to them in attaining such understanding, smoothing the path to implementation, and tailoring the process to fit organizational requirements.

Method and Data Sources

Material for the study was gathered principally from questionnaires sent to 481 organizations that either (1) have sent personnel to zero-base planning and budgeting programs conducted by the American Management Associations and/or (2) are known to have implemented zero-base planning and budgeting systems. Two hundred twenty-three enterprises (46 percent) returned the questionnaires and/or participated via phone interviews. The two largest groups of respondents were planners and financial officers.

A letter covering a set of questionnaires was sent to each organization. The first questionnaire sought such background information as description of the enterprise; annual sales or dollar throughput; total asset level; number of employees; age of the organization; indication of when awareness of ZBB first arose; whether the technique was adopted and, if so, whether it is still in use; how long it has been in use; and where in the organization it is being used. It also requested copies of the ZBB forms in use and the latest annual financial reports. The second questionnaire sought information on implementation of the ZBB system; it asked for the title of the respondent, the reasons for implementing the process, the effects of implementation, the advantages and disadvantages of the process, the amount of time implementation took, the problems encountered, and other information. The mailing was followed up by telephone calls to encourage completion of the questionnaires and timely submission of the ZBB forms in use and annual reports.

In addition to the survey questionnaires, the following information sources were employed: the American Management Associations' Library, the New York City Library, the Library of Congress, the Lockheed Retrieval Service Information Systems Laboratory, the Stanford Business Library, and the University of Utah Library.

It was assumed that zero-base budgeting was established in a responding organization when four of the six criteria described by Peter Pyhrr[1] in his book had been met. The six criteria used to determine the existence of ZBB are as follows:

- Circulation of a letter or memorandum from the chief executive officer announcing the implementation of zero-base budgeting.
- Assignment of a person or a task force to implement the process.
- Existence of a zero-base budgeting manual or procedures document.
- Establishment of a decision package form.
- Existence of a hierarchical ranking process and completed ranking forms.
- Allocation of resources by the process.

Summary of Findings

The following summary gives highlights of the findings:

1. A little more than half of the respondents engaged in the process have known about ZBB for over two years; a little less than a third of those have used ZBB for over two years.

2. The largest single class of users of ZBB within the responding group are manufacturers.

3. The majority of the organizations implementing ZBB are large; 76 percent of the sales generating firms are over $100 million in size, and 51 percent are over $500 million; 59 percent of the nonprofit groups had over 1,000 employees.

4. Of 95 organizations that have implemented or are planning to implement ZBB, 33 (35 percent) are in the planning stage, 57 (60 percent) have completed at least one budgeting cycle, and 5 (6 percent) have stopped using the technique.

5. The most significant objectives for implementing ZBB were (in declining order) to better allocate resources, to improve decision making, and to facilitate planning; the least important objective was to reduce costs or personnel.

6. Of the implementing respondents, 94 percent reported that objectives were fully-to-fairly well achieved; only 6 percent reported that objectives were poorly or not at all achieved.

7. The objectives that were best achieved were to facilitate planning, to improve decision making, and to better allocate resources. The least achieved objective was to reorganize.

8. Of the implementing respondents, 55 percent reported some degree of shift in resources; 23 percent reported no shift; and 23 percent were uncertain whether a shift had taken place or not.

9. The impact of ZBB on corporate profitability was judged to be of some value by 45 percent of respondents answering the question; 11 percent found the impact insignificant or not valuable, and 44 percent were uncertain.

10. Organizations implementing ZBB tended to implement at all organizational levels simultaneously (48 percent did so). The breakdown of those implementing ZBB on a restricted level was as follows: 25 percent implemented the system in headquarters, 13 percent at the division level, and 15 percent in departments.

11. During the first year of implementation, ZBB greatly increased the time and effort required to prepare budgets. During the current year, however, 36 percent reported that the time and effort required either increased only slightly or remained the same; 62 percent reported that it decreased either slightly or considerably.

The balance of this report consists of five sections. Section 2 traces the development of ZBB from its inception to current applications and contrasts the method with other budgeting methods. Section 3 presents the characteristics and responses of organizations implementing ZBB. Section 4 discusses special needs and considerations in implementing ZBB, and Section 5 discusses some benefits and limitations of the process. The report proper is followed by the Appendix, References, and Bibliography.

2
The Zero-Base Budgeting Process

Budgeting has long been a major problem for managers. Internal competition for funds has always been difficult to deal with, and high assurance that funds have been allocated to the organization's best interests hard to come by. Consequently, the search for better methods of allocating and controlling the expenditure of funds has always had a place on every manager's list of priority interests.

Definition of Terms

Over the years, the search has produced a wide range of techniques—among them incremental budgeting, comprehensive budgeting, planning program budgeting, and zero-base planning and budgeting systems. A brief description of budgeting as a general process and of each of the techniques follows:

- *Budgeting.* The process of allocating resources to selected activities or programs. A financial budget is simply a sum of money dedicated to a specific line of activities or accomplishments.

- *Incremental Budgeting.* Early budgeting methods did little to bring into question the assumptions and intentions underlying the allocation of funds. Incremental budgeting was developed as a step in that direction and to provide a bridge between planning and controlling. The method involves analysis of the additional values to be derived from an additional expenditure before it is authorized.[2] However, the process does not require an examination of the budget item itself; it is assumed that the previous year's activities will continue more or less throughout the budget year.

- *Comprehensive Budgeting.* Comprehensive budgeting goes one step further by requiring analysis of *all* budgetary expenditures—those already established as well as those proposed. Here's how Maurice Stans, budget director under President Eisenhower, described comprehensive budgeting:

> "Every item in a budget ought to be on trial for its life each year and matched against all the other claimants to our resources."[3]

The comprehensive approach is to review all expenditures for effectiveness in achieving the organization's goals. Two varieties of the technique are the planning-programming-budgeting system (PPB) and zero-base budgeting (ZBB).

- *Planning-Programming-Budgeting System.* The PPB system was developed during Robert McNamara's term in the Department of Defense. The system relates three elements: the establishing of desired outcome(s) (planning), the structuring of methods to achieve the outcome(s) (programming), and the allocating of funds needed to attain the outcome(s) (budgeting).[4] Charles L. Schultze, Director of the United States

Bureau of the Budget in 1965, described the PPB system as having six elements: (1) careful identification and examination of goals and objectives in each area of government activities; (2) analysis of a given program's output in terms of the objectives set for it; (3) measurement of total programming costs for several years into the future; (4) extension of objectives and programs beyond annual budgets to long-term objectives; (5) analysis of alternatives to find the most efficient and least costly ways of reaching program objectives; and (6) establishment of analytic procedures that would add to the systematic nature and formalization of the budget review process.[5] His description shows that the PPB system is program-oriented, entails cost/benefit analysis, and has a long-range horizon.

• *Zero-Base Budgeting.* Zero-base budgeting emerged from the effort to tighten the coupling between justification and allocation. Peter Pyhrr defines ZBB as follows:

> "An operating, planning, and budgeting process which requires each manager to justify his entire budget request in detail from scratch and shifts the burden of proof to each manager to justify why he should spend any money at all. This approach requires that all activities be identified in "decision packages" which shall be evaluated by systematic analysis in rank order of importance."[6]

Thus, while the statement shows that zero-base budgeting is a form of comprehensive budgeting, it also shows the method to go much further in the demand for analysis and proof of funding need than do other versions of the type.

The terms *sunset budgeting* and *sunset review*, also often heard these days, refer to reviews and analyses being performed in government agencies to determine whether the merits of a given program justify continuing it at the same, higher, or lower levels than its existing level or terminating it altogether.[7] However, sunset budgeting or review is a legislative process linked to Congress's role in authorizing programs and agencies. ZBB, in contradistinction, is primarily a form of executive decision-making and, in government, is linked to the manner in which *agencies* prepare budgets for review. In government, the two methods are associated because both the executive and the legislative branches are involved in the budgetary process. In the private sector, however, top management serves both of these functions, so zero-base budgeting in the private sector stands on its own feet.

Short History of ZBB

As could be assumed, the concept of zero-base budgeting has been around a lot longer than the current surge of interest in it might indicate.

In 1924, E. Hilton Young wrote:

> "It must be a temptation to one drawing up an estimate to save himself trouble by taking last year's estimate for granted, adding something to any item for which an increased expenditure is foreseen. Nothing could be easier, or more wasteful and extravagant. It is in that way obsolete expenditure is enabled to make its appearance year after year, long after reason for it has ceased to be."[8]

Despite the cogency of Mr. Young's remarks, large-scale employment of zero-base budgeting did not occur until nearly forty years later.

U.S. Department of Agriculture

In 1962, The United States Department of Agriculture became the first agency to try ZBB on a large scale.[9] Adoption of ZBB forced the agency into three practices: (1) justification of the need for agency activity and programs without reference to congressional mandates or past practices, (2) justification of the requested level of expenditure based on need, and (3) justification of the cost of the program from zero.

Aaron Wildavsky, Chairman of the Department of Political Science at the University of California in Berkeley, and Arthur Hammond, teaching fellow in psychology at the University of Michigan, studied in detail the application of zero-base budgeting in the Department. They found that nearly all of the agency's managers had great difficulty in thinking about budgets or budgeting free of their ties to legislative mandates or past commitments. The managers persisted in justifying programs, at least in part, by referencing existing legislation —despite the instructions they were given that such justification was not valid. Further, budgets conforming to the instructions seldom were submitted. Time, apparently, was a serious constraint; no one was able to read through and evaluate all the materials submitted.

Another limitation was the lack of workload measures and similar information needed to translate effort into dollars and to cost out the programs. The lack also made it difficult to relate costs and benefits in meaningful ways.

Wildavsky and Hammond concluded that ZBB as applied in the Department of Agriculture failed to achieve its objectives. They commented:

> "Comprehensive budgeting vastly overestimates man's limited ability to calculate, and grossly underestimates the importance of political and technological constraints."[10]

However, they did qualify this conclusion because their study was confined to a single department for only a year.

Although Wildavsky and Hammond arrived at a rather dim conclusion, they noted that nearly half the people interviewed commented favorably on the technique after it was over. Many felt that ZBB was a logical way to budget and claimed to have learned much about their areas of responsibility during the experiment. Wildavsky and Hammond also noted that for the first time in many years the Secretary of Agriculture attended the Department's budgeting hearings, where he made it known that he considered budgeting to be of primary importance. As a result, interest in budgeting rose to new heights in the Department.

Those who expressed negative feelings toward ZBB felt that the workload involved was excessive, too little learning was involved, and nothing had changed as a result of their efforts. Wildavsky and Hammond recommended following the incremental approach, with attention focused on activities that did not change from year to year. Certain programs, they advised, could be subjected to the technique every few years—thus avoiding the burdens of taking a comprehensive approach during every budget cycle.

The Move into Industry

Although ZBB did not take strong hold in government, the private sector soon picked up the technique. The first corporate experience was that of Texas Instruments Incorporated.

The need for zero-base budgeting was first recognized by Texas Instruments during the preparation of its 1969 annual budget.[11] Management decided after a series of ineffective budget meetings that a system to incorporate the answers to the three basic questions was needed as an integral part of the budget process: (1) What are the goals and objectives of the units of organization being budgeted for? (2) What type of expenditures should be anticipated for the next year's budget? and (3) What are the projected shifts and workload requirements between the organizational units? The result was implementation of zero-base budgeting on a trial basis in the staff and research divisions for the 1970 budget cycle.

The adoption of the procedure moved much of the burden of traditional budget analysis from the president to unit managers. Favorable results of the experiment convinced Texas Instruments' president, Pat Haggerty, to require zero-base budgeting for all support activities throughout Texas Instruments.

Some of the benefits reportedly derived by Texas Instruments from adoption of the technique included: (1) better participation of first-line supervisors in forming their budgets; (2) increased efficiency in the evaluation of proposals and allocation of resources to the various divisions and departments; (3) ranking of proposals so that changes in an allocation level require only an examination of marginal proposals and not establishment of a new budget; (4) a closer matching of resources to potential profit contributions; (5) reduction in the number of forms required for budgeting (the old method of budgeting required twelve different forms, whereas the zero-base budgeting technique required only two—a decision package form and a ranking form).

The technique was implemented by Peter Pyhrr, Budget Director of Texas Instruments Incorporated, who later wrote an article on the subject for the *Harvard Business Review* (November-December, 1970). The article attracted wide attention and the technique was quickly picked up by several corporations. Many companies now employ the method, including such corporate giants as Boeing Co., Xerox Corp., BASF, International Harvester, Eastern Airlines, Owens-Illinois, General Dynamics Corp., Rockwell International Corp., and Westinghouse Electric Corporation. Smaller corporations implementing the technique include Parsons & Whittemore, Inc., Gerber Products Co., Allied Van Lines, Inc., Combustion Engineering Inc., and Dillingham Corp. Utilities that have implemented the process include Florida Power & Light Co., Southern California Edison Co., and New York Telephone Co. In the public sector, zero-base budgeting has been adopted by the Energy Resource Development Agency, the Federal Home and Loan Bank Board, the Food and Drug Administration, the General Accounting Office, the States of Florida, Arkansas, California, Georgia, Idaho, Illinois, Missouri, Montana, New Jersey, New Mexico, Rhode Island, Tennessee, and Texas, and the cities of of Grange, Texas; Wilmington, Delaware; Salt Lake City, Utah; and Genesee County, New York. Among the service organizations that have implemented zero-base budgeting, Blue Shield of Virginia and the American College of Obstetricians and Gynecologists stand out.

Experience of the State of Georgia

In 1970, Jimmy Carter was elected Governor of Georgia. His central campaign issue was the need to reorganize the executive branch of government, and he began making plans to reorganize it upon his election. He employed Peter Pyhrr from Texas Instruments Incorporated to help implement zero-base budgeting as a step toward accomplishing his reorganizational goal. On January 11, 1972, Governor Carter introduced the new budgeting system in his state. In an address to the General Assembly of Georgia, he outlined five benefits to be expected: (1) the system would identify 100 percent of each function performed by an agency; (2) it would show the costs and benefits associated with each proposed expenditure; (3) expenditures would be evaluated on merit alone; (4) future changes in expenditures that had been given priority ranking and approved would not require recycling of budget inputs; and (5) the system would rationalize the budgeting process by (a) compelling agency managers to submit proposed expenditures only after accomplishments to date had been evaluated and (b) enabling the Governor's Office to more accurately and efficiently rank budget proposals, reduce the number of budget proposals coming to the Governor's Office, and adjust budgets more easily and realistically.

A study of the zero-base budgeting process as implemented within the State of Georgia was reported in an unpublished dissertation by George Minmier.[12] After conducting an intensive survey, Minmier concluded that ZBB has both advantages and disadvantages.

Advantages. The first advantage Georgia realized was the establishment of a financial planning phase prior to preparation of the year's budget. Before ZBB was introduced, financial planning was conducted concurrently with budgeting—a procedure that prevented a clear separation between proposal merit and funds availability. The implementation of ZBB gave the state the guidelines it needed to satisfactorily meet its goals and objectives with its limited financial resources.

The second advantage was an improvement in the quality of management information—giving the Governor, department heads, and budget department specialists greater insight into the functions of the state government.

The third advantage was increased involvement of- personnel in the State's budgeting process, with a corresponding rise in understanding.

Disadvantages. The major disadvantage of ZBB as established in Georgia was that preparation of the budget took more time and effort than it had previously.

The second disadvantage was the seeming ineffectiveness of the decision package ranking to force changes in the level of funding.

The third disadvantage was the contention that the new budget system to date had not significantly improved the efficiency of allocation of the State's financial resources.

After stating the pros and cons, Minmier concluded that "on balance, the implementation of zero-base budgeting appears to have served the best interests of the State of Georgia."[13]

Why Zero-Base Budgeting?

Traditional (or incremental) budgeting is based on the assumption that relationships underlying budgeting processes are understood—particularly those surrounding the production function. Economically, the production function can be defined as the relationship that expresses the transformation of inputs (traditionally land, labor, capital, and technology) into outputs (goods and services). When the relationship of inputs to output levels is understood, the incremental budgeting process works quite well. For example, the chemical process that produces phonograph records prescribes (1) the input of direct materials such as polystyrene or polypropylene, (2) direct labor components related to the technological level of the plastic extruding machine, and (3) the other cost components of energy usage and depreciation of capital equipment. This production process transforms the inputs into phonograph records. The amounts of the inputs are generally fixed in terms of their proportion to the number of outputs (records) wanted; they are fixed by standards developed by the production function. Standard costing techniques allow us to calculate any variance in this proportion and isolate the particular input or inputs responsible. And the process works quite well; whenever we have an understanding of underlying economic relationships, the traditional budgeting process and the standard costing system serve well.

Budgeting is difficult, however, when clear relationships between inputs and outputs are lacking. Where inputs are of the nature of the number of accountants or attorneys, the level of public relations activity, and so on, it is difficult to see how much in the way of personnel and effort will be required to produce a product or service for the marketplace. ZBB was designed specifically to deal with this problem. The technique can be simply defined as allocation of resources by results, meaning that we specify the results that we wish to obtain within each of the organizational units and then allocate the resources needed to attain them. One can then decide through a priority ranking process which of the results/resource units are most important within some overall budgeting constraint.

Two things have happened during the past several decades to make the traditional budgeting process obsolete in some applications. The first was the massive shift from production to services; around 70 percent of the gross national product is now generated by service-related industries or enterprises. The second was the increasing amount of overhead and administrative expenditures within manufacturing organizations—many of which were prompted by government regulation in such areas as pollution control, workers' safety, and anti-trust measures.

General Features of ZBB

The two basic steps of zero-base budgeting are:

1. *Developing decision packages*, which involves analyzing and describing each discrete activity, both current as well as new, in one or more decision packages.
2. *Ranking the decision packages*, which involves evaluating and ranking the packages that have been developed in priority order, employing cost/benefit analysis or subjective evaluation.

The decision package identifies the reasons for performing an activity, the consequences of not performing the activity, measures of performance, alternative courses of action, and costs of the alternatives chosen. The key to the zero-base budgeting process lies in the identification and evaluation of alternatives for each activity. Two types of alternatives are presented: The first consists of the different ways a given function can be performed and the second the different levels of effort at which the function can be performed. The first decision to be made selects the way a particular result will be achieved, and the second determines the resources to be used in achieving that result. Thus we have allocation by results, and that allocation increases as results increase.

Developing Decision Packages

The first step in developing decision packages is to identify the decision unit or units within an organization and the manager who will begin to write packages for one or more units. Such a unit may be defined as a particular cost center, a group of people, a particular product or service provided or received, an objective of an expenditure such as lease payments, a capital expenditure or expenditures, or a program to reduce costs or enhance revenue. The issue is essentially an organizational quesrion: How are we going to organize to achieve the individual unit results that will accomplish the mission of the overall organization?

The second step in developing decision packages is to decide whether the results of the decision unit will be continued, eliminated, or changed—and whether new results may arise. The third step is to develop optional ways of achieving results by "playing with" different arrangements of the various activities involved. A fourth step is to decide the level below which the result cannot be accomplished—that is, a minimum or threshold level of accomplishment required, below which it is pointless to try for the result. We may then increase expenditures from one level of effort to another in order to achieve a greater result along one or more dimensions: increased quantity, increased quality, or reduced time.

The manager carries the process through the five steps and then incorporates the resultant information into a decision package, so named because it states the set of decisions he has made in allocating resources towards his desired results. (Examples of decision packages are shown in the Appendix.)

Ranking Decision Packages

Once the decision packages have been developed by the various managers, each preparing packages for one or more decision units under his responsibility, the packages can be ranked. Ranking involves arranging the packages in priority order on the basis of cost/benefit analysis or subjective evaluation. The first step is for a manager to rank all the packages within his individual jurisdiction. The second step is to submit to the next level of management the set of ranked packages attached to a ranking sheet that summarizes the ranking decisions. The manager at that level takes packages from each subordinate manager, merges into one list those packages above predetermined cutoff levels, reranks the packages below those levels, and then sends all the packages—merged and reranked—up to the next managerial level.

Determining the cutoff percentage for packages at each managerial stage of the process is made by considering the number of managerial levels in the organization and the amount of authority granted to each. The ranking process then continues from ranking to reranking through each managerial level until the process reaches either the chief executive officer or a budget committee. Here, the overall organizational ranking is listed, so that all decision packages developed within the organization are given priority numbers from one through the total number of packages developed (small organizations might need only a few hundred, while very large organizations would need several thousand). A cutoff line is then drawn at the point where the package costs above the line add up to the total sum earmarked for the period's budgets. Decision packages above the cutoff line will be funded; those below, dropped.

The ZBB process does not require the complete quantification of all costs and benefits. It gets away from this by using an ordinal ranking process for analyzing the decision packages. All that needs to be known is that package No. 1 is better than package No. 2, that No. 2 is better than No. 3, and so forth—not that No. 1 is twice as good as No. 2, or that No. 2 is four times as good as No. 3.

The Objectives of the System

Zero-base budgeting is essentially a decision-making process. Just as planning is essentially a process of making decisions in the present to govern an organization's future behavior, so budgeting is a process of governing its future resource usage. Zero-base budgeting arose from a need to more closely link intended results with the use of resources. Zero-base planning and budgeting did not arise in a vacuum; it grew out of many attempts to cope with the deficiencies of traditional budgeting methods.

The Foundations of ZBB

The theoretical underpinnings of the zero-base planning and budgeting concept are microeconomics and decision making under conditions of uncertainty.

Microeconomics is primarily concerned with an organization's internal processes. Break-even analysis, in which fixed and variable costs are separated, is an extension of microeconomic theory. The purpose of separating the two costs is to establish a functional relationship between them. Traditional budgeting methods work well where fixed and variable cost relationships can be clearly and conveniently established. Zero-base budgeting works better where such relationships cannot be so clearly established.

The other concept underlying zero-base planning and budgeting—decision-making under conditions of uncertainty—postulates that while there is no certainty in this world, decisions nonetheless have to be made; yet while uncertainties of every sort add to the difficulty of making any decision, information is always available to reduce the uncertainty. Therefore, any methodology for obtaining and analyzing data that resolve uncertainty can add to the optimality of decisions.

Implications

The ZBB process highlights the need for—and therefore encourages the adoption of—cost/benefit analysis to add information to the allocation decision although, as previously mentioned, the technique does not require the complete quantification of all costs and benefits.

Zero-base budgeting also holds implications for management styles. In a recent *Harvard Business Review* article (July-August, 1976), Henry Mintzberg discusses the differences between what he calls the planner type of individual and the manager type. Mintzberg says that if we take a close look at each type, we will see that they are quite different. He says that *planners* tend to be thinkers of the more comprehensive and strategic kind, that they're more concerned with future events and behavioral issues; *managers,* on the other hand, tend to be more financially based, day-to-day, operating-oriented, logical-flow-through, step-by-step kinds of thinkers. Yet despite these basic differences, company plans are almost always formed out of contributions from both types. The different documentations produced by planners and managers for inclusion in plans are often difficult to reconcile. Again, the zero-base technique solves a difficulty; the new way it provides for making decisions fosters integration of the outputs that derive from different management styles, orientations, and organizational interests.

Zero-base planning and budgeting is particularly helpful in integrating organization planning activity with financial planning activity. Financial planning is more concerned with the procurement and application of resources. Organization planning is primarily concerned with strategy development and the identification of results. Zero-base planning and budgeting makes flexible organizing necessary. The focus is upon a re-examination of the organization at each funding period to determine what organizational implications are posed by the funding granted. Financial planning seldom covers organizational considerations, and organizational planning rarely offers a consideration of the financial flows. The zero-base process forces us to look at what the organization is going to be in terms of its results from the resources to be used.

Logan Cheek's book, *Zero-Base Budgeting Comes of Age*, carries the current thinking about zero-base budgeting through implementation.[14] He discusses how to organize the zero-base budgeting process, the alternative methods for ranking decision packages, the integration of the ZBB process with the regular planning process, the selling of the concept and the ideas it generates, how to use the process to foster innovation, top management's role in implementing the process, and how to overcome common concerns during the implementation period.

Dealing with Negative Aspects of the Name

To some managers, ZBB lacks positive associations, and many suggestions for changing the name have been made. Respondent Martin Merel of the Tiger Leasing Group suggests changing the name *zero-base budgeting* because "it has a negative connotation." He suggests, in its place, *priority resource planning.* A number of enterprises have changed the name to *activity-base planning, program budgeting,* and *zero-base planning and budgeting* (the last one being by far the most popular).

The dislike of the prevailing name may have arisen from past applications. When ZBB first began to take hold, several firms used it to reduce personnel and costs. Today, as experience and sophistication in using ZBB build up, those two objectives have become the least important among ZBB objectives—where, indeed, they are recognized at all.

Changing the name to *zero-base planning and budgeting* makes a good deal of sense because the technique necessarily involves program planning, activity-based planning, and resource priority planning. The change is realistic; sound budgets are always born of effective planning efforts, and that fact more than any other ought to be reflected in the technique's name. Note that, in the balance of this survey report, the initials ZBB stand for zero-base planning and budgeting.

3

Characteristics and Responses of Organizations Implementing ZBB

The survey encompassed 481 organizations, 223 of which responded by filling in questionnaires and/or giving information over the telephone. Of the respondents, 95 (43 percent), had used or were planning implementation of zero-base budgeting. Of these 95, 57 had employed ZBB for at least one cycle, 33 were planning implementation, and only 5 had stopped using the method. (See Exhibit 1.)

EXHIBIT 1. Organizations by stage of ZBB implementation.

	Number	Percent
Implemented and using ZBB	57	60%
Planning ZBB implementation	33	35
Implemented and stopped using ZBB	5	5
	95	100%

Types of Organizations

The 95 users of ZBB were classified by the following organizational categories: (1) profit-oriented (80 percent)—of which 6 (6 percent) were diversified, 36 (38 percent) were manufacturing firms, 9 (9 percent) were in finance/services, 9 (9 percent) were utilities, and 16 (17 percent) were "other"; and (2) nonprofit—of which 19 (20 percent) were education/health-care organizations, 8 (8 percent) were government/military, 9 (9 percent) were "other."

Exhibit 2 shows the organizational class of the three groups of respondents—(1) implemented and using ZBB, (2) planning to implement ZBB, and (3) implemented and stopped using ZBB.

Size of the Implementing Organizations

In Exhibits 3 and 4, respondents have been segregated by size—the 67 profit-oriented entities (78 percent) by sales volume, and the 19 nonprofit organizations (22 percent) by number of employees. Profit making organizations were placed within four sales volume classes: under $25 million, 5 (7 percent); $25 million to $100 million, 11 (16 percent); $100 million to $500 million, 17 (25 percent); and over $500 million, 34 (51 percent). Nonprofit organizations were distributed within four classes: 1 to 500 employees, 3 (16 percent); 501 to 1,000 employees, 5 (26 percent); 1,001 to 5,000 employees, 5 (26 percent); and over 5,000 employees, 6 (32 percent). These exhibits show that large organizations—both public and private—have implemented ZBB to a greater extent than have small organizations.

Age of the Organizations

In Exhibit 5, respondents are classified by the number of years they had been operating: under 10 years, 22 (24 percent); between 10 and 50 years, 36 (39 percent); and over 50 years, 35

EXHIBIT 2. Class of organizations having implemented or planning to implement ZBB.

	Implemented and using ZBB		Planning ZBB Implementation		Implemented and Stopped Using ZBB	
	Number	Percent	Number	Percent	Number	Percent
Profit oriented						
Diversified	5	9%	1	3%	0	0%
Manufacturing	23	40	10	30	3	60
Services/Finance	2	4	6	18	1	20
Utility	4	7	5	15	0	0
Other	11	19	5	15	0	0
Subtotal	45	79%	27	81%	4	80%
Nonprofit						
Education and Healthcare	4	7%	4	12%	0	0%
Government/ Military	7	12	2	6	0	0
Other	1	2	0	0	1	20
Subtotal	12	21%	6	18%	1	20%
TOTAL	57	100%	33	100%	5	100%

(38 percent). The exhibit further separates respondents into the three groups previously mentioned.

Of these respondents answering the age question, there were more than three times as many in the over-ten-year group as in the under-ten-year group—and all five organizations that had stopped using ZBB were more than ten years old. (It was interesting to note among the survey returns that there were no ZBB implementers in the more mature industries—automobile, steel, oil.)

Length of Time Since Discovering and Implementing ZBB

In Exhibit 6, the organizations are classified (1) by the length of time they have been aware of ZBB—1 year, 11 (19 percent); 2 years, 15 (26 percent); and over 2 years, 31 (54 percent)—and (2) by the number of years ZBB has been installed—1 year, 25 (46 percent); 2 years, 13 (24 percent); and over 2 years, 16 (30 percent). As can be seen, 80 percent of the establishments responding to the questions have been aware of

EXHIBIT 3. Size (by sales volume) of implementing firms.

	Implemented ZBB		Planning ZBB		Stopped Using ZBB	
Annual Sales	Number	Percent	Number	Percent	Number	Percent
Under $25 million	2	5%	2	10%	1	25%
$25 to $100 million	8	19	3	15	0	0
$100 to $500 million	12	28	4	20	1	25
$500 million and over	21	49	11	55	2	50
TOTAL	43	100%	20	100%	4	100%

EXHIBIT 4. Size (by number of employees) of non-profit organizations that have implemented or plan to implement ZBB.

Employees	Number	Percent
1-500	3	16%
501-1000	5	26
1001-5000	5	26
Over 5000	6	32
TOTAL	19	100%

ZBB for two years or more, but only 54 percent have implemented the technique.

Where Implementation Took Place

Exhibit 7 presents the organizational level of ZBB implementation: headquarters level, 12 (25 percent); divisional level, 6 (13 percent); departmental level, 7 (15 percent); and all levels, 23 (48 percent). About half of those answering this question implemented ZBB throughout the organization. In such organizations, top management obviously views the implementation decision as an all-or-nothing proposition.

Titles of Respondents

Respondents were classified into four categories: presidents, 6 (19 percent); financial officers, 16 (24 percent); planners, 27 (40 percent); and all others, 18 (27 percent). These figures are displayed in Exhibit 8. The data provided in the sample population may be slightly biased by a large percentage of planners versus the other positions sampled in each organization.

Most Significant Reasons for Implementing ZBB

The respondents were asked to choose the most significant reasons for implementing ZBB in their organizations. Five were commonly cited; the rest were unique and are grouped as miscellaneous. Of the five, one reason—to reorganize—received no responses for the highest significance. The other reasons, in order of significance, were (1) to better allocate resources, 17 (30 percent); (2) to improve decision making, 14 (25 percent); (3) to facilitate planning, 11 (20 percent); and (4) to reduce costs or personnel, 7 (12 percent). These results are shown in Exhibit 9.

The data seem to contradict some of the literature, which often reports ZBB as a cost cutting or personnel reducing technique. As Exhibit 9 shows, respondents have that purpose far down on their list of priorities. However, ZBB is a method for making the resource allocation decision—specifically to allocate by results.

Degree of Achieving the Purposes for Implementing ZBB

Exhibit 10 shows the degree to which the purposes of implementing the ZBB process were achieved. (Of the 57 respondents on this matter, all had completed one ZBB cycle and, of these, five had stopped using ZBB. The respondents were allowed to rate as many purposes as applied among five purposes listed.) Obviously, the effectiveness of ZBB is supported by the data in the exhibit—with 94 percent of the purposes of the responding organizations achieved to some degree.

The responses shown in Exhibit 10 are further broken down—by purpose—in Exhibit 11. There,

EXHIBIT 5. Ages of organizations implementing ZBB.

Number of Years Operating	Implemented ZBB		Planning ZBB		Stopped	
	Number	Percent	Number	Percent	Number	Percent
Under 10 years	11	20%	11	34%	0	0%
10–50 years	25	45	9	28	2	40
Over 50 years	20	36	12	38	3	60
TOTAL	56	100%	32	100%	5	100%

we see that the most effective achievement of purpose was to facilitate planning (97 percent of those rating this purpose responded *extremely well, well, or fairly well);* the next most effectively achieved purpose was to improve decision making (also 97 percent); then came to better allocate resources (94 percent); then to reduce costs or personnel (91 percent); then to accomplish some other purpose (89 percent).

EXHIBIT 6. How long organizations have been aware of ZBB compared with when ZBB was implemented.

	Aware		*Implemented*	
Number of years	Number	Percent	Number	Percent
1 year	11	19%	25	46%
2 years	15	26	13	24
Over 2 years	31	54	16	30
TOTAL	57	100%	54	100%

EXHIBIT 7. Organizational level of ZBB implementation.

Organizational Level	ZBB Implementation	
	Number	Percent
Headquarters	12	25%
Division	6	13
Department	7	15
All	23	48
TOTAL	48	100%

EXHIBIT 8. Implementing respondents by title.

Title	Respondents	
	Number	Percent
President	6	9%
Financial Officer	16	24
Planner	27	40
Other	18	27
TOTAL	67	100%

EXHIBIT 9. Most significant reason for implementing ZBB.

Purpose	Implementing ZBB	
	Number	Percent
To Better Allocate Resources	17	30%
To Improve Decision Making	14	25
To Facilitate Planning	11	20
To Reduce Costs/Personnel	7	12
To Reorganize	—	—
Miscellaneous	7	13
TOTAL	56	100%

EXHIBIT 10. Degree of achieving the reasons for implementing ZBB.

Degree of Achievement	Purpose Achieved	
	Number	Percent
Extremely Well	37	25%
Well	64	43
Fairly Well	40	26
Poorly	6	4
Not at All	3	2
TOTAL	150	100%

Resource Shifts Resulting from ZBB Implementation

Respondents were asked to determine whether resources were shifted within the organization as a result of ZBB implementation. Here's how the responses of those who answered broke down: large shift of resources, 4 (8 percent); some shift of resources, 25 (47 percent); no shift of resources, 12 (23 percent); or uncertain of any resource shifts, 12 (23 percent). Exhibit 12 presents these data. The high level of "uncertain" and "no shift" answers is explained by the fact that almost 50 percent of respondents using ZBB have done so for less than two years.

Impact of ZBB Implementation on Corporate Profitability

Asked to determine the value of ZBB implementation in improving corporate profitability,

EXHIBIT 11. Breakdown of specific purposes in implementing ZBB, with individual achievement levels.

Purpose Achieved	Extremely Well		Well		Fairly Well		Poorly		Not at All	
	#	%	#	%	#	%	#	%	#	%
To Better Allocate Resources	8	22	17	27	8	20	1	17	1	33
To Facilitate Planning	10	27	17	27	4	10	1	17	—	—
To Reduce Costs/ Personnel	3	8	10	16	18	45	2	33	1	33
To Reorganize	2	5	2	3	2	5	—	—	1	33
To Improve Decision-Making	10	27	15	23	7	18	1	17	—	—
Other	4	10	3	5	1	2	1	17	—	—
TOTAL	37	100	64	100	40	100	6	100	3	100

respondents answered as follows: extremely valuable, 4 (9 percent); somewhat valuable, 16 (36 percent); not valuable, 5 (11 percent); or uncertain, 20 (44 percent). These data are displayed in Exhibit 13.

Effect of ZBB Implementation on Time and Effort Required in Budget Preparation

Exhibit 14 reports responses to the question asking for an assessment of ZBB implementation upon time and effort required in budget preparation. Respondents were asked to assess the time and effort required during the first year: increased considerably or slightly, 44 (92 percent); remained the same or decreased slightly, 4 (8

percent). They were also asked how ZBB impacted their time in the most recent year of using the technique: increased considerably or slightly, 5 (13 percent); remained the same, 10 (26 percent); or decreased slightly or considerably, 24 (62 percent).

The respondents were further queried on where resource shifts came from and where they went. Most of the responses were across the board (for example, marketing to maintenance, manufacturing to engineering, engineering to maintenance, finance to administration, manufacturing to finance, administrative support to marketing, personnel to other services). However, about a third did indicate a shift into research and development (for example, from

EXHIBIT 12. Resource shifts resulting from ZBB implementation.

Resource Shift	Implementing ZBB	
	Number	Percent
Large shift	4	8%
Some shift	25	47
No shift	12	23
Uncertain	12	23
TOTAL	53	100%

EXHIBIT 13. Impact of ZBB implementation on corporate profitability.

Value	Impact on Profits	
	Number	Percent
Extremely valuable	4	9%
Somewhat valuable	16	36
Not valuable	5	11
Uncertain	20	44
TOTAL	45	100%

Effect on Time and Effort	First Year		Current Year	
	Number	Percent	Number	Percent
Increased Considerably	35	73%	1	3%
Increased Slightly	9	19	4	10
Remained the Same	3	6	10	26
Decreased Slightly	1	2	17	44
Decreased Considerably	–	–	7	18
TOTAL	48	100%	39	100%

administrative, marketing, manufacturing, and other departments into research and development and with new product development). One of the benefits of ZBB implementation seems to be a movement of funds from current expenditures toward spending for the futurity of the enterprise.

4 Special Needs and Considerations in Implementing ZBB

Organizations about to embark on installing ZBB should be aware of some special considerations and needs entailed. (Where the following recommendations spring from survey responses, this is specifically noted; otherwise, the recommendations are the author's.)

The Need for a Comprehensive Plan

In the last analysis, the effectiveness of ZBB rests squarely on the existence of a comprehensive, far-reaching, integrated plan of the kind often referred to these days in the private sector as a business plan. To fulfill its own objectives, ZBB must take place within the framework of a clear and cogent statement of purposes, goals, and strategies.

The Need for a Detailed Implementation Plan

Beyond that, a plan for installing ZBB needs to be developed. Respondent James Caldwell of Monsanto Company counsels to "allow plenty of time, don't rush, plan very carefully." The immediate purpose of introducing ZBB—to change managerial behavior—is very difficult to achieve. Therefore, each installation step must be thoughtfully planned for, scheduled, and followed up.

Half of the organizations answering the question on level of implementation adopted an all-or-nothing approach and initiated ZBB throughout the organization simultaneously; the other half installed ZBB on a trial or pilot basis first. In many of the latter cases, headquarters was selected—that is, the controller's office, administration, personnel, and similar staff units rather than line units.

On balance, the across-the-board approach appears to have found greater favor—avoiding, as it does, the "Why me?" problem. But where the one-part-of-the-organization-at-a-time method is adopted, the first trial should be horizontal—not vertical. It should be noted here that the advisability of implementing ZBB throughout the organization varies from one type of organization to another. In a manufacturing organization, ZBB applies to only 15-25 percent of the total budget; the remainder is kept on standard costing. But in a service organization, ZBB applies to nearly all of the budget.

The Implementation Plan

An implementation plan should include the following steps: (1) Prepare a ZBB proposal for top management; (2) answer the implementation policy questions; (3) develop ZBB manual forms and implementation schedule; and (4) sell and communicate the ZBB process to all levels of management.

1. *Prepare a ZBB proposal for top management.* The ZBB proposal to top management should include a statement on the kind and level of

Date	Action
December 16	Distribution of zero-base budget instructions to all applicable agencies and departments.
December 16 to 18	Training of departmental staff in zero-base budgeting concepts and procedures.
December 19 to January 14	Documentation and analysis by departments and agencies of current program operations.
January 14	Preparation by department heads of their proposed consolidated rankings (for departments or agencies containing more than one budget unit).
January 14 to 21	Review by the chief executive officer of rankings and service level descriptions and, as necessary, consultation with department heads before giving tentative approval.
January 14 to January 30	Completion by departments of service level analyses and review and completion of final ranking.
January 30	Submission by the departments of completed analysis and ranking forms, accompanied by a letter briefly summarizing the basis or rationale for the selection of service levels and the order of ranking.
February 2 to 20	Review of budget detail by the CEO, followed by a budget hearing with department heads and their staffs.
February 20 to 25	Formulation by the chief executive officer of the initial consolidated ranking for the agency as a whole.
February 25 to March 9	Review (and appropriate modification) by the chief executive officer of the initial consolidated ranking with department heads.
March 9 to 16	Recommendation to the CEO of proposed rankings for modification and approval.
March 17 to 31	Preparation of the budget message by the CEO. Preparation of the final budget document for submission to the Board.
April 1	Presentation by the CEO of the budget message to the Board.
April 1 to May 31	Review by the Board of the annual operating budget plan and the annual capital budget. Balancing of the budget. Adoption of the capital program and approval of the operating and capital budgets.

commitment required—commitment to involvement, to time and effort, to planning and control, to excellence. The results discussed in this survey report may prove helpful in making such a proposal. And you may want to ask that your top management call other top managers in organizations that have implemented ZBB.

2. *Establish implementation policies.* Start by asking the following questions:

- To what degree will ZBB be implemented—headquarters, divisions, departments, all? Will it replace or run parallel to the current budget system?
- What planning assumptions and strategic objectives does top management need to give lower-level managers—on, for example, products or services to be marketed, wage and salary increases, cost adjustments, and ways of handling personnel reductions?
- What guidelines need to be issued for developing and ranking the decision packages? What figures should be used for the current year's cost? Should optional packages be written? How are the minimum or threshold and the cutoff levels going to be defined? Should there be a formal review process?

3. *Develop the ZBB manual, forms, and implementation schedule.* Section 2 of this report can help in developing the ZBB manual. And the sample forms in the Appendix should help in designing the ZBB forms. Exhibit 15 gives an example of an implementation schedule.

4. *Sell and communicate the ZBB process to all levels of management.* Communication of the process to top management centers on the word *commitment*—again, to involvement, to time and

The Chicago office of Peat, Marwick, Mitchell & Co. recently published survey responses of 391 business executives and government officials who participated in a seminar on basic zero-base budgeting concepts. Because of the current debate over whether the zero base process will improve budgeting mechanics, the responses of the participants are summarized below. The respondents were 68 percent from the private sector, 17 percent from the public sector, and 15 percent from healthcare organizations.

	Yes	No	Don't Know
Planning and budgeting will be more important to realizing our goals during the next few years than ever before.	93%	2%	5%
Our planning and budgeting system generally meets the needs of most management levels.	47%	42%	11%
Our current budgeting system is formalized and relies heavily on the impact of planning assumptions and strategies provided by top management.	51%	41%	8%
Certain aspects of zero-base budgeting would improve our present budgeting procedures.	81%	2%	17%
We are likely to seriously consider implementation of a revised budgeting system using the ZBB approach or elements of it.	47%	14%	39%
President Carter's administration will succeed in implementing zero-base budgeting in a significant portion of our federal government.	16%	46%	38%
If President Carter's administration does implement zero-base budgeting in important federal agencies, government efficiency will be improved significantly.	47%	20%	33%
Do you believe extensive implementation of ZBB will reduce federal income taxes?	19%	62%	19%

*Reprinted with permission from Managerial Planning, Vol. 26, No. 1 (July-August 1977), p. 40.

effort, to planning, to control, to excellence. Communication of the process to middle management should include the following points:

- Bilateral agreements, which are established between each superior and subordinate linkage. When budgets are cut and resources reduced, the agreement is on the reduction of a particular effort or service as well as the reduction of dollars.
- Proactive posture, which allows managers to request as large an amount of resources as they desire to accomplish the results they want. Instead of being boxed in by the budget before deciding which results are going to be achieved (reactive), the manager determines the results he or she wants and then requests the budget (proactive).
- Opportunity for options, which enables managers to go after results the way *they* want, without being limited by the previous year's restrictions.
- Documentation of competency, which occurs because his or her input is documented in black and white for future reference.

Developing Decision Packages

The forms used in zero-base planning and budgeting need to be designed specifically for each organization with consideration of the following:

1. *The nature of the planning process in the organization*—specifically, long-range or strategic planning. Since ZBB is a technique for allocating resources toward results, questions of how results are established, who decides what results are to be considered, and where results are documented arise.

2. *Whether the current budget mechanism will be totally replaced or paralleled by ZBB.* The

answer affects the kind and number of formats to be used in documenting budgets.

3. *The accounting system in the organization.* Questions here include: To what degree will the data be broken down from decision package totals to specific line-item categories? How will the actual-to-budget data be treated? What computerization requirements are presented? How often will the data be compared—monthly, quarterly, or other?

All information displayed on the decision package forms must focus upon the result. According to Douglas Nagoshi of Dillingham Corporation, "Packages must be clear, lucid, and have supporting back-up detail." The result must be defined in terms of the quantity of production or service produced, the level of quality required, and the time frame required for accomplishment.

Walter Peterson, Coast Guard, says, "ZBB shouldn't stand on its own; it must be integrated into your other programs—MBO, for example."

Once the decision packages have results pinpointed, each activity statement should specify what is required to achieve the result. Options or alternatives available to achieve the result also need to be stated. Several respondents indicated that alternatives or options were difficult to get. Yet a key managerial ability is that of creating options to accomplish the organization's results.

The result specified for one decision unit (encompassing one or more decision packages) must be holistic and discrete to avoid situations reflecting the use of part or fractional employees. Several respondents found using such fractions to be a nightmare. Aside from the difficulty of having to tell an employee, "John, only 60 percent of you can come to work tomorrow," the communication process breaks down and performance eventually falters.

There are two ways of dealing with the problem: (1) Amalgamate the decision unit with one at a higher level so that only whole people are encompassed, or (2) write a decision package summary that reflects the varying functions or projects performed by one person or a group of people so that the decision packages can be written for a group of whole people.

Some respondents suggested establishing guidelines to limit the number of decision packages.

Packages written for most organizations average three to eight people, or $20,000 to $100,000 in resources. Of course, the manager writing packages should have the freedom to develop packages for his results without constraints on the method he uses or the way he breaks them down.

However it is cut, the writing of a decision package needs to be explicit and definitive, containing all the information required for top management to make a decision. Although the resource allocation is always made with uncertainty, information carefully supplied by subordinate managers can help reduce the degree of uncertainty.

Objectives, for example, must be quantified; thus *better* or *more* becomes *10 percent over last year's level.* And *an improved chance for success* would become *only an 8 to 10 percent probability of failure.* Miles Stejskal of International Harvester Co. says: "Simplify format and working of decision packages. Try to reduce long explanations and descriptive narrative."

The development of decision packages by managers at cost centers or departmental levels can create interfunctional conflict. Such is the case with the data processing department, which services other departments. Accordingly, many organizations have added an initialing procedure to the decision package for such contingencies—a procedure that requires interdependent departments to sign each other's decision packages.

Ranking of Decision Packages

Clear guidelines and criteria for ranking decision packages must be established. Since the views of lower-level managers sometimes conflict with those of higher-level managers, the overall ranking must be reviewed and approved by top management and understood by all.

Decision packages can be ranked by first placing them into one of three categories: In the first group would be all those that are legally or functionally required. There would be no disagreement in the final ranking process over their eminence as the organization's highest or most necessary priority. The second group would include all packages that are merely dreams. Obviously, these packages would never be able to muster the support required for their ratification.

The third and last group, perhaps the largest, would include all packages that cannot be easily classified into either of the first two groups. This last group would then be ranked from top to bottom, one by one. The first group would be placed on the top of the list without worry about order of listing because the budget constraint would be far below this group. The second group would not have to be ranked at all unless there is a possibility that the packages in it may be funded.

A major problem reported by some respondents was a difficulty in ranking packages that may differ widely in results or in dollars. This is not an easy problem to solve, but some respondents have minimized it by requesting the rational consolidation of small packages (where logical and feasible) into larger units and/or the breakdown of oversized packages into smaller ones.

It is just this kind of choice that management must face up to—not bury or overlook. Somehow the funding decision *will* be made. The question is whether it will be made with or without the manager's input.

The Need for Integration

Plans for installing ZBB must include an understanding that ZBB must dovetail with the accounting system involved. Larry Helber of Bendix Corp. was one of several respondents who described this: "There is a need, at the outset, to plan how to convert decision packages to the standard budget account code so that variances can be compared." At issue is the tracking of ZBB information. About half of the respondents who have implemented ZBB use it as a decision tool, not a control tool. The other half use ZBB information to control by tracking the actual-to-budget accounting data—actual amounts against amounts that were allocated to each decision package.

Once the decision packages have been ranked, the packages need to be returned to the managers who wrote them. This feedback process is essential to the manager who wrote the package so that he can see where his request for funds was ranked and can ask the question: Why?

The Need for Education

In keeping with the commonplace that every change creates resistance, a good deal of resistance to ZBB arises after the system is installed. Therefore, any program for implementing ZBB should include preparatory training. According to respondent Gene Nordling of Tektronix, Inc., the necessity is for "ZBB education at all levels before anything is put into effect."

The key to gaining early acceptance of the program probably rests in the idea that ZBB is a technique developed by managers to help them manage better. The technique should be promoted as a method for simplifying managerial life. And it needs to be promoted; though managers talk a good deal about ZBB these days, many of them consciously or unconsciously resist it because they suspect that implementing it will erode their authority, reduce "flexibility," and so on. On the contrary, however, a number of managers have discovered that a properly designed and implemented ZBB system helps them fulfill their own and corporate objectives more effectively.

The ZBB system should not be sold merely as a new managerial gimmick or cure-all for budgeting problems, however. As David DeWind of the United California Bank wrote in response to this survey, "It should be presented as part of one's on-going budgeting system; it must be integrated into the existing budget and planning process— the five-year plan, the accounting structure, and so forth."

Education for implementation should also focus on the need for patience. As is common with complex techniques, the results often take longer to realize than expected. John Bombino, Director of Finance and Administration for United Nuclear Industries, Inc., suggests, "You must explain to managers that this (ZBB) is not an instant-success solution; it will take two or three years to reap the full benefits."

5

Benefits and Limitations of the ZBB Process

Like any other managerial technique, ZBB has both benefits and limitations. (These observations are drawn from the author's experience except where otherwise indicated.)

Benefits

First, let's look at the benefits.

Linking Results with Allocations

As previously mentioned, zero-base planning and budgeting does a better job of connecting resource allocation to results than any other method currently in use. It forces a closer examination of assumptions related to allocations than any other method. Other budgeting methods often allocate resources on percentage extrapolations or applications of rules of thumb. ZBB forces the examination because it starts with nothing and requires specific results to be stipulated before allocation is allowed. Thus attention is forced upon results rather than upon dollars. By the time attention is paid to resource allocations, the results have been weighed and tested.

The process of allocating funds under the ZBB concept requires that the results be ranked one against another. Since this ranking controls how much they will get, managers are forced to support their results and the resources they think they will need to achieve them.

Zero-base planning and budgeting facilitates the altering of allocations as planning changes are presented. The technique provides wider contact with and commitment to the allocation process. Under other budgeting methods, budgets are prepared primarily by a firm's financial division and then sent to managers throughout the organization. Managers then struggle to make their portion of the corporate plan (which they also got elsewhere) fit their budgets—a process entailing a lot of grumbling and open or surreptitious negotiating.

Fostering Commitment and Creativity

Traditional budgeting processes too often weaken either managerial creativity or commitment to budget objectives. By contrast, ZBB fosters creativity and commitment because it requires the manager to state what he is going to achieve and what he will need in the way of resources to achieve it. He is not likely to forget that *he developed* the objectives and *he won* the resources to achieve them as he works toward the results *he said he could attain.*

Gaining Decision Making Power

Another benefit relates to the use of power. Within every organization, power generally emanates from the chief executive officer and dissipates downward hierarchically within the organization. But, as most managers learn the hard way, there is also an informal organization that often has enough power to change the way decisions are supposed to be made. No budgeting process can, by itself, totally offset the informal power structure. But the increased rationality that ZBB builds into the decision making process (by developing information that reduces uncertainty about the decision itself) can go some distance in overcoming the decision warping influence of the informal organization. The manager who does a top-notch job of providing such information will ultimately gain power because his decisions are almost bound to have impact on the decisions made at upper levels.

Increasing Feedback on Decisions

To manage well, every manager needs to see the results of his decisions in a timely fashion. ZBB provides such feedback to the manager who wrote them. Seeing how their packages were ranked, managers can discuss with their superiors why they were so ranked and gain a better understanding of the factors influencing allocation decisions. The limitation here lies in the commitment of management to follow through on the feedback process.

Benefits by Type of Organization

Some benefits of the ZBB process depend upon the type of organization involved. Large firms, for example, tend to benefit by getting an increased amount of relevant information about the nature of their organization and where their money is being spent. One consequence of this is that they discover areas of potential cost savings.

Small firms tend to get their benefits from improved decision making. The decision making process tends to become more formal and rational with the implementation of ZBB—an occurrence of enormous importance to small firms that generally cannot afford the specialization of large firms.

Government organizations tend to benefit by realizing a methodology for reorganizing. Using zero-base planning and budgeting enables them to more clearly decide which results are going to be achieved and who should be made responsible for attaining them. Characteristically resistant to change, government organizations will find in ZBB a change strategy that focuses on the most critical area in government: funding.

Service organizations realize their greatest benefit in the form of improved interaction in the decision making process. The ranking process brings the management team together and generates interaction around results and resource allocation decisions.

Planning

ZBB improves the quality of planning because it (1) provides a mechanism for contingencies whereby once or twice a year new packages are added, others are deleted, and some are rewritten, after which all are reranked—reported by Roger Van Cleve of Allied Van Lines, Inc.; (2) facilitates the matching of resources with objectives—reported by Dennis E. Hiser of Texas Instruments; (3) permits resources to be shifted into higher payout areas and provides what Robert Welch of Ohio Bell Telephone Co. calls "an important bridge between MBO and standard budgeting"; and (4) gives managers, according to G. P. Segner of Westinghouse Electric Corp., a "better understanding of objectives and how to apply the budget accordingly."

Organizing

ZBB helps the organizing function by (1) clarifying resource responsibility; (2) defining lines of responsibility—according to Miles Stejskal of International Harvester Co.; (3) eliminating duplications and overlaps of responsibility and authority; and (4) increasing managerial awareness of responsibilities—reported by W. W. Phelps of Combustion Engineering Inc. C. Leonard Bedsaul of The American College of Obstetricians and Gynecologists sums it up as follows: "People know who does what, when, and how."

ZBB improves the communication process—from one managerial level to another, up and down in the organization. It also improves cooperation among managers and provides a good tool for feedback on managerial decision making.

Control

According to Michael F. Walsh, of the National Association of Blue Shield Plans, ZBB enhances the control function by (1) helping people understand what others are doing, (2) providing more logical and better organized documentation, (3) providing a method for tracking and evaluating performance, (4) indicating the priorities for critical control, and (5) permitting valid comparisons of projects.

Decision Planning

ZBB improves the decision making process by (1) placing decisions in priority order—Douglas Nagoshi of Dillingham Corp; (2) giving management more options or alternatives to select from—Henry H. Goldman of Norris Industries; (3) justifying the reasons for shifting funds, and (4) achieving a bilateral agreement between superior and subordinate regarding the decision. Dr. Morton Ehrlich of Eastern Airlines sums up ZBB in this area as being "excellent for helping with decision making for planning budgets, programs, projects, and schedules."

Management Development

Several organizations reported that ZBB had added to their management development efforts. Management visibility is improved because the competent manager's competency is documented. The information provided by ZBB is "especially valuable for new managers," reports Tony Maro of FMC Corporation. Both the new and the seasoned manager can better understand their jobs and how their roles help accomplish organizational goals. "Participation in the ZBB process can be invaluable in training and development," says Joseph Tully of McGraw-Hill.

Savings (In Cost, In Personnel)

William Bagot of Union Carbide Corp. reports that ZBB can serve as a "vehicle for cost reductions." And according to Martin Merel of the Tiger Leasing Group, ZBB triggers the "realization that some functions cost more than they are worth." Cost areas within organizations are identified. Nonessential areas, especially those built into previous budgets, are quickly identified. Daniel R. Pealer of Cooper Energy Services reports that ZBB "permits doing things cheaper while maintaining the quality of performance." The ZBB process "encourages cost consciousness" among managers, reports Larry Helber of Bendix Corp.

Better Understanding of the Budget/Planning Process

ZBB also leads to a better understanding of the budgeting and planning process: (1) It gives "a closer overview of the whole budget," states Bernard Rome of AMF Incorporated; (2) Frank Alcorn of Owens-Illinois, Inc. reports "greater management involvement; budgets have become a matter of concern to all managers."

Limitations

The zero-base planning and budgeting process has several limitations. The first relates to objectives; ambiguous or nebulous objectives make it almost impossible to allocate resources rationally.

Not a Technique for All Reasons

The second limitation is in application; ZBB is not a technique that can be universally applied. In manufacturing, for example, technology determines the mix and levels of inputs, and standard costing provides the basis for budgeting—so there is no need for zero-base methods. On the other hand, ZBB is applicable and needed where standard costing and traditional budgeting techniques do not work well—in, for example, service, support, and other staff functions. Traditional budgeting methods apply primarily to manufacturing and other production-oriented functions.

The Novelty Doesn't Last

The third limitation of the ZBB process is true of all budgeting processes; it, too, can become quite mechanical. Although zero-base planning and budgeting brings into use new terms, new forms, and a new framework for making decisions, the novelty does not assure continued pursuit of the technique's benefits.

Appendix
Samples of
Decision Packages from
the Watervliet Paper Company

Decision Package (Level 1)

Decision Package	WATERVLIET PAPER CO.	Code: F-7	Rank: 12

Objective or Activity:

Product Development and Technical Service

Level 1 of 3

Department: TECHNICAL

Division/Section: MAIN LAB.

Desired Results:

1) Develop specialties and other new grades of paper.
2) Assist Production and Sales in technical areas.

Description of Activity:

1) Research new products and processes for grade development.
2) Product testing, problem solving and quality control of incoming materials.
3) Routine monitoring of effluent system.

Resources Required	Current Year	Budget Year		
		This Level	Accum.	% of Cur. Yr.
Personnel (Sal./Hrly.)	2 / 2	1 / 1	1 / 1	
Salaried (Non-Union)$	55,053	29,955	29,955	54
Hourly (Union)	30,497	17,500	17,500	57
Variables	7,105	5,600	5,600	79
Total	92,655	53,055	53,055	57

How and When Accomplished:

1) Conduct 75 projects/year on current and new products with 10 percent probability of success.
2) Plan and direct 70 plant trials/yr. for prod. dev., cost reduction and problem solving.
3) Assist Production on emergency problems.
4) Assist Sales in developing new specialties.
5) Monitor quality of pulp on a spot basis (3 times a week), 20 moisture checks and 10 beater runs per year.
6) Daily monitoring of waste discharged to effluent system.

Other Options/Alternatives to Achieve Same or Partial Results:

Eliminate Main Lab. and have necessary functions performed by the operating departments. Savings: $38,820.

Advantages of Retaining Activity:

1) Continued growth and development of Watervliet grade structure.
2) Minimum loss of production due to technical problems.
3) Continued cost reduction and quality improvement.
4) Assurance of a quality pulp supply.
5) Assurance of meeting water discharge standards.
6) Eliminate need to upgrade other personnel to perform above duties.

Consequences if Activity is Eliminated:

1) Quality Control would have to cover all mill testing.
2) Production departments would have to do their own research, trial work, and trouble shooting.
3) Product development would have to be accomplished through Sales and Production on a direct basis.

Prepared by: L. R. Beeman	Date: 2/15/77	Approved by: M. F. Stibal	Date: 2/17/77

Decision Package	WATERVLIET PAPER CO.	Code: F-7	Rank: 43

Objective or Activity:

Product Development and Technical Service

Level 2 of 3

Department: TECHNICAL

Division/Section: MAIN LAB.

Desired Results:

1) Develop more specialties and other new grades of paper.
2) Assist Production and Sales in technical areas.

Resources Required	Current Year	Budget Year		
		This Level	Accum.	% of Cur. Yr.
Personnel (Sal./Hrly.)	2 / 2	1 / 1	2 / 2	
Salaried (Non-Union)$	55,053	26,420	56,375	102
Hourly (Union)	30,497	15,300	32,800	108
Variables	7,105	2,100	7,700	108
Total	92,655	43,820	96,875	105

Description of Activity:

1) Research new products and processes for grade development.
2) Product testing, problem solving and quality control of incoming materials.
3) Limited customer contact for (1) & (2).
4) Routine monitoring of effluent system.

How and When Accomplished:

1) Conduct 110 projects/year on current and new products with 10 percent probability of success.
2) Plan and direct 100 plant trials/yr. for prod. dev., cost reduction and problem solving.
3) Assist Production on emergency problems.
4) Assist Sales in developing new specialties.
5) Monitor quality of all incoming pulp (2 hrs./day) and 43 moisture checks and 18 beater runs per year.
6) Daily monitoring of waste discharged to effluent system.

Other Options/Alternatives to Achieve Same or Partial Results:

Reduce Lab. force to one salaried and one hourly employee and retain above services at about 2/3 the current level.

Advantages of Retaining Activity:

1) Continued growth and development of Watervliet grade structure.
2) Minimum loss of production due to technical problems.
3) Continued cost reduction and quality improvement.
4) Assurance of a quality pulp supply.
5) Assurance of meeting water discharge standards.
6) Eliminate need to upgrade other personnel to perform above duties.

Consequences if Activity is Eliminated:

1) Quality Control would have to cover all mill testing.
2) Production departments would have to do their own research, trial work, and trouble shooting.
3) Product development would have to be accomplished through Sales and Production on a direct basis.

Prepared by: L. R. Beeman Date: 2/15/77	Approved by: M. F. Stibal Date: 2/17/77

Decision Package	WATERVLIET PAPER CO.	Code: F-7	Rank: 67

Objective or Activity:

Product Development and Technical Service

Level 3 of 3

Department: TECHNICAL

Division/Section: MAIN LAB.

Desired Results:

1) Develop additional specialties and other new grades of paper.
2) Assist Production and Sales in technical areas.

Description of Activity:

1) Research new products and processes for grade development.
2) Product testing, problem solving and quality control of incoming materials.
3) Limited customer contact for (1) and (2).
4) Routine monitoring of effluent system.

Resources Required	Current Year	Budget Year		
		This Level	Accum.	% of Cur. Yr.
Personnel (Sal./Hrly.)	2 / 2	1 / 0	3 / 2	
Salaried (Non-Union)$	55,053	11,000	67,375	122
Hourly (Union)	30,497	∅	32,800	108
Variables	7,105	1,250	8,950	126
Total	92,655	12,250	109,125	118

How and When Accomplished (Additional chemist 3rd quarter):

1) Conduct 150 projects/year on current and new products with 10 percent probability of success.
2) Plan and direct 135 plant trials/yr. for prod. dev., cost reduction and problem solving.
3) Assist Production on emergency problems.
4) Assist Sales in developing new specialties.
5) Monitor quality of all incoming pulp (2 hrs./day) and 60 moisture checks and 24 beater runs per year.
6) Daily monitoring of waste discharged to effluent system.

Other Options/Alternatives to Achieve Same or Partial Results:

Reduce Lab. force to two salaried and two hourly employees and retain above services at about 2/3 the current level.

Advantages of Retaining Activity:

1) Continued growth and development of Watervliet grade structure.
2) Minimum loss of production due to technical problems.
3) Continued cost reduction and quality improvement.
4) Assurance of a quality pulp supply.
5) Assurance of meeting water discharge standards.
6) Eliminate need to upgrade other personnel to perform above duties.

Consequences if Activity is Eliminated:

1) Quality Control would have to cover all mill testing.
2) Production departments would have to do their own research, trial work, and trouble shooting.
3) Product development would have to be accomplished through Sales and Production on a direct basis.

Prepared by: L. R. Beeman	**Date:** 2/15/77	**Approved by:** M. F. Stibal	**Date:** 2/17/77

References

1. Peter A. Pyhrr, *Zero-Base Budgeting* (New York: John Wiley & Sons, 1973).
2. Verne B. Lewis, "Towards a Theory of Budgeting," *Public Administration Review*, Vol. 12, No. 1 (Winter 1952), p. 42.
3. Aaron Wildavsky and Arthur Hammond, "Comprehensive Versus Incremental Budgeting in the Department of Agriculture," *Administrative Science Quarterly*, Vol. 10, No. 3 (December 1965), p. 142.
4. Bertram M. Gross, "The New Systems Budgeting," *Public Administration Review*, Vol. 29, No. 2 (March-April 1969), p. 116.
5. Charles L. Schultze, *The Politics and Economics of Public Spending* (Washington: The Brookings Institution, 1968), pp. 19-23.
6. Peter A. Pyhrr, "Zero-Base Budgeting," an unpublished speech delivered to the International Conference of the Planning Executives Institute, Hilton Hotel, New York, May 15, 1972.
7. U.S. Senate Sunset Act of 1977, Bill S.2., p. 11.
8. A. E. Buck, *The Budget in Governments of Today* (New York: MacMillan, 1934), p. 172.
9. Aaron Wildavsky, *op. cit.*
10. *Ibid.*, p. 157.
11. Sub-committee on Intergovernmental Relations Committee on Government Operations, U.S. Senate, *Compendium of Materials on Zero-Base Budgeting in the States*, January 1977, p. VIII.
12. George S. Minmier, "An Evaluation of Zero-Base Budgeting as a Tool for Planning and Control of Discretionary Costs in Government Institutions," an unpublished Ph.D. dissertation, University of Arkansas, 1974.
13. George S. Minmier and Roger H. Hermanson, "A Look at Zero-Base Budgeting—The Georgia Experience," *Atlanta Economic Journal*, Vol. 26, No. 4 (July-August 1976), p. 11.
14. Logan M. Cheek, *Zero-Base Budgeting Comes of Age* (New York: AMACOM, 1977).

Bibliography

1. Anthony, R. N., and Herzlinger, R. E., *Management Control in Non-Profit Organizations* (Homewood, Illinois: Dow-Jones Irwin, 1976).
2. Bensehel, Jane G., "Zero-Base Management," *International Management*, Vol. 32, No. 1 (January 1977), pp. 36-37.
3. Buck, A. E., *The Budget in Governments of Today* (New York: MacMillan, 1934).
4. Carter, President Jimmy, "Zero-Base Budgeting," *Nation's Business*, Vol. 65, No. 1 (January 1977), pp. 24-25.
5. Cheek, Logan, *Zero-Base Budgeting Comes of Age* (New York: AMACOM, 1977).
6. Davis, Otto A.; Dempster, M. A. H.; and Wildavsky, Aaron, "A Theory of the Budgeting Process," *American Political Science Review*, Vol. 60, No. 3 (September 1966), pp. 529-547.
7. Dean, Burton V., "Conceptual Problems and Implementing Zero-Base Budgeting," U.S. Department of Commerce, Spring Symposium, New Directions and Resource Allocation: The Role of Zero-Base Budgeting and Program Evaluation, March 16-17, 1977.
8. Garbutt, Douglas, and Minmier, George S., "Incremental, Planned-Programmed and Zero-Base Budgeting," *Public Finance and Accountancy*, Vol. 1, No. 11 (November 1974), pp. 350-357.
9. Granof, Michael H., and Kinsel, Dale A., "Zero-Based Budgeting: Modest Proposal for Reform," *Federal Accountant*, Vol. 23, No. 4 (December 1974), pp. 50-56.
10. Gross, Bertram M., "The New Systems Budgeting," *Public Administration Review*, Vol. 29, No. 2 (March-April 1969), pp. 113-137.
11. Hayward, John T., "Buzz Words Galore!" *Government Executive*, Vol. 8, No. 9 (September 1976), pp. 19 and 21.
12. Hill, Walter D., *Implementing Zero-Base Budgeting—The Real World*. Oxford, Ohio: The Planning Executives Institute, 1977.
13. "Zero-Based Budgets Offer Data, Spending Control," *Industry Week*, Vol. 188, No. 2 (January 12, 1976), pp. 48-50.
14. Leininger, David L., and Wong, Ronald C., "Zero-Base Budgeting in Garland, Texas," *Management Informations Service*, Vol. 8, No. 4A (April 1976), pp. 1-6.
15. Leven, Merwin, "Zero-Based Budgeting," *Boardroom Reports*, Vol. 5, No. 24 (December 30, 1976), pg. 14.
16. Lewis, Verne B., "Toward a Theory of Budgeting," *Public Administration Review*, Vol. 12, No. 1 (Winter 1952), p. 42.
17. MacFarlane, John A., "Zero-Base Budgeting in Action," *Chartered Accountants*, Vol. 109, No. 6 (December 1976), pp. 28-32.
18. McGinnis, James F., "Pluses and Minuses of Zero-Base Budgeting," *Administrative Management*, Vol. 37, No. 9 (September 1976), pp. 23-23 and p. 91.
19. Merewitz, Leonard, and Sosmick, Stephen, *Budget's New Clothes: A Critique of Planning—Program—Budgeting and Benefit-Cost Analysis* (Santa Monica, California: Rand Corporation, 1971).
20. Miller, Karl A., "Zero Budgeting Works in Yonkers, N.Y.," *Government Exccutive*, Vol. 9, No. 11 (January 1977), pp. 39-40.
21. Minmier, George S., "An Evaluation of Zero-Base Budgeting as a Tool for Planning and Control of Discretionary Costs in Government Institutions," an unpublished Ph.D. dissertation, University of Arkansas, 1974.
22. Minmier, George S., and Hermanson, Roger H., "A Look at Zero-Base Budgeting—The Georgia

Experience," *Atlanta Economic Journal*, Vol. 26, No. 4 (July-August 1976), pp. 5-12.

23. Murray, Thomas J., "The Tough Job of Zero Budgeting," *Dun's Review*, Vol. 104, No. 4 (October 1974), pp. 71-72, 128, and 130.

24. Nadler, David A., and Pecorella, Patricia A., "Differential Effects of Interventions in Organizations," *Journal of Applied Behavioral Science*, Vol. 11, No. 3 (July-August 1975), pp. 348-366.

25. Peterson, Walter E., "Zero-Base Management System," *Military Engineer*, Vol. 68, No. 445 (September-October 1975), pp. 371-373.

26. Pyhrr, Peter A., "Zero-Base Budgeting," *Harvard Business Review*, Vol. 48, No. 6 (November-December 1970), pp. 111-121.

27. Pyhrr, Peter A., *Zero-Base Budgeting* (New York: John Wiley & Sons, 1973).

28. Pyhrr, Peter A., "The Zero-Base Budgeting Process," Chapter 9 in *How to Improve Profitability Through More Effective Planning*, edited by Thomas S. Dudick (New York: John Wiley & Sons, 1975).

29. Pyhrr, Peter A., "Zero-Base Budgeting," an unpublished speech delivered to the International Conference of the Planning Executives Institute, Hilton Hotel, New York, May 15, 1972.

30. Pyhrr, Peter A., "Zero-Base Budgeting: Where to Use It and How to Begin," *Advanced Management Journal*, Vol. 41, No. 3 (Summer 1976), pp. 4-14.

31. Schultze, Charles L., *The Politics and Economics of Public Spending*. Washington, D.C.: The Brookings Institution, 1968.

32. Searfoss, D. Gerald, and Monczka, Robert M., "Perceived Participation in the Budget Process and Motivation to Achieve the Budget," *Academy of Management Journal*, Vol. 16, No. 4 (December 1973), pp. 541-554.

33. Singleton, David W.; Smith, Bruch A.; and Cleveland, James R., "Zero-based Budgeting in Wilmington, Delaware," *Governmental Finance*, Vol. 5, No. 3 (August 1976), pp. 20-29.

34. Stein, Herbert, "How About Zero-Based Revenue?" *The Wall Street Journal*, Vol. 189, No. 1 (January 3, 1977), p. 17.

35. Stonich, Paul J., and Steeves, William H., "Zero-Base Planning and Budgeting for Utilities," *Public Utilities Fortnightly*, Vol. 98, No. 6 (September 9, 1976), pp. 24-29.

36. Sub-Committee on Intergovernmental Relations, Committee on Government Operations, U.S. Senate, "Compendium of Materials on Zero-Base Budgeting in the States," January, 1977.

37. Vancil, R. F., Texas Instruments, Incorporated; Harvard Business School Case 9-172-054; September 1975.

38. Wildavsky, Aaron, and Hammond, Arthur, "Comprehensive Versus Incremental Budgeting in the Department of Agriculture," *Administrative Science Quarterly*, Vol. 10, No. 3 (December 1965), pp. 321-346.

39. Wright, Norman H., Jr., "Zero-Base Planning and Budgeting," *Management World*, Vol. 5, No. 10 (October 1976), pp. 24-26.